DEDICATION

I would like to dedicate this book of remembrance to my mother, Joann Dunn Sparks. I hope that somehow, someday, she can realize how much I love and appreciate her. I am confident that God, as our loving Heavenly Father, has his own way of evening up scores for those who had such a hard time on this earth.

Mom, I am looking forward to seeing you in heaven. Thank God I found the Savior and gave my life to him. Thank you for loving and caring for us.

Mama in Younger, Better Days and Grandma Dunn

ACKNOWLEDGMENTS

I wish to thank the following for help and support in the production of this remembrance book.

Writer-Phyllis Amos Lane

Artist-Kenneth Schrimsher

Pastor-Rev. Leonard Shubert

Wife-Leanna Sparks

Sister-Patty Thompson

Most of all, I want to thank God for making it possible for me to share these remembrances.

PROLOGUE

In her "Little House..." book series, author Laura Ingalls Wilder prefaces several stories with the phrase, "If I had a remembrance book I would write in it of the time when..." As the reader laughs and cries with Laura through her remembrances he learns that through *all* of life's experiences there is woven a thread common to every human. That thread is the encompassing care of an omnipotent Heavenly Father. God's loving care and gracious mercy are evident in the book of remembrances you are about to read.

The telling of remembrances is a practice God instituted early in the Holy Scriptures. When the Israelites were brought out of Egyptian bondage they were instructed to establish a tradition of celebrating the Passover feast. The two-fold purpose of this regularly repeated celebration was to remind Israel of God's delivering power and to preserve and bear the record of His deliverance from generation to generation.

The sharing of a Christian's personal story serves the same dual purpose. It reminds the teller and the Christian reader of God's goodness. At the same time, it acquaints a reader who does not know the Lord with the benefits of accepting God's love. How a person chooses to exercise his free will regarding God determines both the development and the outcome of his story. *Real* life does not begin until that point in time when one *chooses* to acknowledge God and to accept His loving care. The earlier one admits that God, as Creator, has authority to order life, the more of God's blessings can be claimed. By the same token the sooner one submits to the Lordship of Jesus Christ, the more Satan's pitfalls can be avoided. Only in God's family are defeats made triumphs. Only God can make dreams come true. There is plenty of testimony in "Living Life in a Living Hell" to indicate the vast difference between the miserable life he suffered before Christ and the abundant life he has enjoyed since Jesus entered his heart. Flip's early years without Jesus were disastrous; his current walk with the Lord is full of joy and peace. Your author has made every effort to give glory to God.

Too often a storyteller gets caught up in his own story that he deludes his reader with the notion that living without God can be an exciting adventure. This is very unfortunate for the reader because there is nothing adventurous or exciting about trying to survive without God. In fact, outside of God's family, life is a total disaster and brings misery to the sinner as well as to everyone his life touches. Your author knows these truths very well.

This record of remembrances is not intended to give any place to the devil. Mr. Sparks has absolutely no desire to boast of Satan's deceitfulness or to glory in the sinful condition of a man without God. Rather, this book's only purposes are to point each reader to Almighty God's tender loving care and to display God's gift of everlasting mercy; a gift available to anyone who will receive it by accepting Jesus as savior.

"Living Life in a Living Hell" is an accurate description of the two sides of life-one of which each of us must choose. Picture life as a phonograph record (vinyl disc on which music was recorded in earlier years of electronics). While one side is our Messiah's terrible suffering and agonizing death, the flip side is our own redemption from the curse of sin. The flip side of life spent in the shadow of Calvary's cross is a life spent in the hopeless desolation of this world. In fact, if life were a phonograph record, side one would hold the greatest love song ever written. All music notation, lyrics, instrumentation, and instructions are found in God's Word, the Bible. Also included in His Word are many arrangements and various renditions of that same love song-God's love for man. "…My God shall supply all your need according to his riches in glory by Christ Jesus." (Philippians 4:19)

Side two of the record of life is filled with the unknown song of destruction. Only the form of destruction is unknown, because God has described the ending of both sides of this record. "For the wages of sin is death, but the gift of God is eternal life through Jesus Christ our Lord." (Romans 6:23)

Hopefully, these remembrances will inform the reader that God's mercy is available to everyone. Furthermore, it is the prayer of this storyteller that each reader will recognize and accept God in order to benefit from His many blessings. As God brought Flip from darkness to light and from despair to hope, He can and will do the same for all who ask and permit Him.

Phyllis Amos Lane

TABLE OF CONTENTS

LIST OF PHOTOGRAPHS AND ILLUSTRATIONS

INTRODUCTION

My name is Jeff Sparks. When I was born, thirty-five years ago, my parents lived on Clover Hill Road in Maryville, Tennessee. My daddy's name was William Wade "Bud" Sparks. He died of heart failure at the age of thirty-nine. My mama, Joann Dunn Sparks, was forty-nine when she was brutally murdered by my brother, Donny.

The doctors and others believed that Donny's act of killing Mama resulted from earlier deprivation and abuse. Daddy used to kick, stomp, and slap us around. There were times when we would have to leave home and go to neighbors for safety. Daddy tried to run us over with cars. He shot at us. Often, he took us in vehicles running over

100 miles per hour. It was really rough growing up this way. It was really scary, too.

The only peace and quiet we ever knew was when Daddy passed out. While he was unconscious, Mama or Ronny would go and get Daddy's billfold. Then we would slip off to the store for candy and cold drinks. With these treats we thought we'd died and gone to Heaven.

Although Daddy's father was an abusive man, his mother, Pearl Myers Sparks, was one of the most beautiful women anyone could ever meet. When we would come in from Ohio, Mamaw would give us a big bear hug no matter what time of night we arrived. It was great coming to Tennessee because of Mamaw. I would ride in the back of that old station wagon looking out the window for red clay dirt and cedar trees. When I saw these East Tennessee wonders, I knew we were almost safe with Mamaw.

In spite of Mamaw's goodness and the protective haven we enjoyed at her house, the generational curse of abuse followed Daddy. It plagued my entire life. I am still battling with some of the scars it caused. Hopefully, this information will help other people not to take the same roads that I took. During most of my adult life I have been disabled because of the way I was raised. The emotional deprivation along with the physical and mental abuse I suffered while growing up made me unable to function with different people successfully enough to hold down a job. I thank God that He healed me of this problem.

All of my brothers have been in prison. They also have mental disabilities resulting from the abuse we received. My sister, I'm glad to say, has not suffered so badly. Patty found Jesus early in life and left home to escape the abuse. She has been blessed. The Lord allowed her to prosper. Patty is the mother of two beautiful children, Shawna and Jonathon. What a difference Jesus makes!

While the love of Jesus was blossoming in Patty's heart, a terrible rage filled mine. This rage permeated my entire being and threatened to consume me until Jesus Christ entered my life. He removed every bit of the rage and replaced it with His love. Thank God for the Blood of Jesus!. My heart is broken every time I hear the song lyrics, "he built a bridge with three nails and two pieces of wood." When I think about how God had to watch as

Jesus, his own Son, was beaten and crucified for my sins, it just blows me away to know that He did it for me. And, God did it for you, too.

My parents married in Tennessee when Mama was only fifteen. She was sixteen when Ronny was born. At that time the family lived on Gilwater Lane in Maryville, Tennessee. Soon after Ronny's birth, the abuse began. It was here, nestled in the picturesque foothills of the Great Smoky Mountains, that our family nightmare started. First, Daddy began kicking and slapping Mama. One abusive act led to another.

Two years after Ronny's birth, Patty was born. Donny was born in 1960 and I was born in 1962. Last, but not least, Jimmy was born in 1964. Times were hard in

Tennessee, so we moved to Ohio trying to survive. Daddy worked hard to support us, but it seemed that the more he tried, the more the devil would plot against him.

In my family everyone had a nickname. Patty became "LuLu." Her nickname was taken from the TV show, "Hee Haw." My older brother Ronny, alias "Bronson," is an avid motorcycle rider. Because Donny jumped in his bed like a frog, Daddy called him, "Frog."

Daddy kept our heads shaved when we were children (before shaved heads were stylish). We all teased Jimmy our youngest brother by rubbing his head and calling him, "Onion." The nickname stuck with him. Daddy was the type of man who hated long hair. I think those short haircuts in childhood evolved into the long hair I wear as an adult. When my head wasn't shaved, Daddy made

Mama put a bowl over it and cut my hair around the bowl. All of the kids wore those ultra-short burr haircuts but only Jimmy was called "Onion" because of his skinned head. My brothers teased me by saying I looked like TV comedian Flip Wilson. Although their teasing made me cry, it gave me the nickname "Flip," which I still carry to this day.

As you read my remembrances, please be encouraged to seek God on a personal basis. Please recognize His loving care for me when I was most unlovable. Most of all, please see the difference Jesus made when I finally invited Him to live in my heart.

"THANKS BE TO GOD FOR HIS UNSPEAKABLE
GIFT!" (2 Corinthians 9:15)

Jeff "Flip" Sparks

Sparks Grandparents and Daddy

Left to Right

Donny "Frog", Moma, Daddy, Ronny "Bronson", Jeff

"Flip", Patty "Lulu", Jimmy "Onion"

REMEMBERANCES

Side Two/ Living Life in a Living Hell

The Beginning of Fear

The first time I ever actually remember being abused by my father was between five and six years old. I heard a vehicle coming down the road. I walked over to the windowsill and raised myself up on tiptoe to see outside. From the window I could see my daddy in that car; an old Dodge with those "Batman Wings" on the back. My daddy was so drunk he couldn't even hold his head up. He backed across the road into a neighbor's driveway, rammed the car back into first gear, drove forward wide open and hit a pick up truck. He was trying to push the truck into the

1

garage with the garage door down. He either passed out or was knocked out when he hit the truck. That day, a fear came over me. I lived in that fear for a long time. I still remember that day. That's when it all started.

I remember another day when we were on the Cincinnati Bridge passing a semitrailer. We were on the sidewalk running about 80 mph. I can remember looking out the window and realizing that I could touch the truck's tire with my finger.

It didn't seem like we had any love in our family. In fact, as far as my father was concerned, there was no love in our family. It was just the hatred and rage that was in his own life on which we had to survive. Without the God of love, how could this fear not rule our lives?

Crystal Gayle

I can remember a time I went to school in New Carlisle, Ohio. I believe I was in the third grade. Believe it or not, Crystal Gayle was my teacher. I remember how I "fell in love" with her. It seemed that if anybody cared, she did. I can remember in third grade I would tell Miss Gayle that I wanted to take dynamite to school and blow everything up.

She would take me to the principal, and he would whip me. I remember that I would have done anything to get her attention. Believe me, with the pranks I pulled, I got that attention! When Miss Gayle became famous, my mama often reminded me that she had been my teacher.

As time went on we moved to Dayton, Ohio. I remember moving back to Tennessee from Ohio early in 1970. My Mamaw died later that year. Things really got bad when we moved back to Tennessee. To get here, my daddy actually sold a brick home he had built. He took $100 for the house in order to have enough gas money to get us home. I said we came back home although Tennessee seemed more of a hellhole than a home. No place seemed like a home. I am just thankful for what God says in the bible that this old world is not our home but just a passing through place. Praise the Lord!

Mamaw's Death

After arriving in Tennessee, we moved into a place off Six-Mile. It was an old house that my uncle owned. I can remember after Mamaw died how my daddy started to drink more and more. He would sit around and listen to old capital gospel music songs and cry like a baby. I've seen him cry for thirty to forty-five minutes at a time. Daddy would listen to that old song:

> Give me the roses while I live
>
> Trying to carry me on.
>
> Useless are the flowers that you give
>
> After the soul is gone.

It is a beautiful old song. Maybe some of you recall it in your own remembrances.

After listening to the songs and crying, Daddy would get his gun out. He would shoot holes in the floor of the

5

house. He would shoot holes in the ceiling. Other times we would actually be going down the interstate when he would rear back, take his foot and kick the windshield completely out of the vehicle. He would shoot holes in the floorboard of the car. We could hear the bullets bouncing of the transmission. We would be in the back of that old station wagon (or whatever we were riding at the time) just crying and begging him to stop… to pull over…to quit hurting us…stop abusing us…to quit beating Mama… We were asking ourselves if and when the abuse would ever stop.

Nerves

At this same place at Six-Mile, Tennessee, there was an old shed I used to crawl under. I remember how I would go there just to get peace and quiet. A place where I wouldn't have to listen to all the stuff going on at home.

I can remember how my stomach would tie up in knots because of my nerves. Imagine, if you can, a young child in this kind of nervous condition. I would quiver and jerk all over because of the abuse my daddy was putting us through. Talk about stress…I needed stress reducers before they became popular health topics. I finally found the greatest stress reducer. His name is Jesus.

Older cousin

It was around this time (1970) that an older cousin was sexually molesting me. At seven years old, I was too young to know how very wrong it was. I had never known

7

anything except abuse and this was just something else to endure. What my cousin would do was to get us smoking pot. I can remember times when I would get so sick that I would crawl on the floorboard of the car. My cousin would give us cigarettes, pot, and other stuff. He played a big role in my life. He was the older person I looked to as my role model.

I can remember riding an old tractor to the store with him to steal cigarettes. He and I spent a lot of time together. Later in life, I found out, to my disappointment, that my cousin was also sexually molesting my brother, Donny. I believe with all my heart that this abuse had a lot to do with the hatred and rage that destroyed Donny and my mother.

Rage

There was a lot of hate in my family. We were never united and we always fought with each other. Even after my daddy died, we would beat each other for forty-five minutes or more at a time. We would get into a fight and beat each other until we would actually be on the ground. I can remember times when I had to drag myself to a water hose to get a drink of water. We would lay there and rest until the rage came back. Then we would get up and go back into the fight again.

That rage we had in our life came from Daddy. I believe with all my heart that my Daddy was a possessed man. At this writing, I am thirty-five years old and I have never known a man that was meaner than my own Daddy. I

9

am sure there may be someone colder and meaner out there but I have never met them.

Roofing business

Donny and I were the two closest members of the whole family. We walked side by side with each other. It started in Ohio while we were young boys shoveling gravel out of a steel-bed dump truck. Working closely with each other led to our closeness. When we returned to Tennessee we continued to work for Daddy. We started a roofing business called Bud and Sons Roofing Company. We would work anywhere from eighty to one hundred and twenty hours per week. I remember while working so hard and long that my legs were sweating and rubbing together causing big welts. I had to take off my shirt and tear it up to put between my legs.

Daddy built a pretty good business with fifteen men working for him. These men were in addition to his sons. We did more roofing than anybody else in Blount County.

Green Paint

I could remember a time when my daddy came in and had several cans of paint with him. He gave each of us a paint brush and told us to paint the trucks. We painted every one of our trucks and cars cow green. I never found out until a couple of years ago why he did that.

Daddy and my brothers were going down the road. There was a vehicle in front of them going too slowly for daddy. My brother, Ronny, was driving. My daddy stretched his foot over and put it on the gas pedal. He held the pedal to the floor until they rammed the other vehicle knocking it over the embankment. After daddy realized what he had done, it shook him up a little bit. His reasoned that all of his vehicles should be painted. So, we painted every vehicle that we had cow green. No one would recognize us now!

No missed chances

My daddy was the type of person that never missed a chance to mistreat us. Once, my older brothers stole some goldfish out of a neighbor lady's pond. My younger brother and I were sitting on the couch while they received their whippings in the next room. Daddy opened the door and saw us sitting there. He ordered us, "get up and come and get one too! I'm going to give you one ahead of time."

You know, when the next time a whipping came, I was not about to tell him that I had already had mine. There was no way!

Daddy never missed a chance to be abusive. One morning he told Ronny to get up but Ronny just laid there. Daddy came into the kitchen and sat down. I knew there was going to be trouble. Daddy stood up, got a twenty dollar bill out of his billfold and put it on the table. He bet Ronny the twenty dollars that he could 'stomp' him. Ronny put his own twenty dollars on the table and they went outside. Daddy ended up with a garden hose and beat Ronny all the way down the road and back. When it was over, Daddy came back inside, took the money and we all went to work just like nothing had happened. It was just another typical morning for us.

We had a dog named Fido. When he was just a pup, his tail was bent in a bus door. The bent tail never bothered Fido but it bothered Daddy. One night Daddy said, "get me a knife, boy". I didn't know why he wanted the knife. I soon found out. Daddy cut Fido's tail off right inside the house. Blood was everywhere! I will never forget poor Fido yelping and crying.

Moonshine

My daddy started making moonshine on Peach Orchard Road. He drove across Knoxville to sell to a friend called Tater.

14

Tater spent time in prison later and eventually became part of the Mafia, but that is another story. He was the type of person my daddy had for a friend.

It was on Peach orchard Road where I started drinking rotgut whiskey. Little did I know that my liver was already being attacked.

We had one hundred head of hog right there where we lived on Peach Orchard Road, probably a mile from the Maryville city limit. The hogs would eat the mash from the whiskey. (Mash is left over when whiskey is brewed and made.)

I can remember the garage building we had was maybe 90'x30'. We had a moonshine still in their that filled up at least half of that entire garage. Small explosions were not uncommon. I can remember sitting there at night scared to death that someone, a monster or something, would come walking through the door. I used to have to sit at the still and watch. Every time a jug would get full, I would have to remove it, put a lid on it, set it aside and put another jug in its place.

The Blast

I will never forget when the still had a huge explosion. I was outside mowing the yard. There was a one hundred gallon propane tank in the garage. When I saw smoke coming from the side of the garage, I ran to see what had happened!

As I walked in the door I saw the hose from the propane tank loose and flying around. I thought daddy was in there. I ran back to the house and hollered, "the garage is on fire and Daddy's in there!"

I will never forget the look on Daddy's face when he jumped up off the couch. He looked at me and gritted his teeth. I thought he was going to knock my head off. Luckily, he had mercy on me as he rushed passed to get outside. When the propane tank blew up, it was reported that the blast rattled windows in downtown Maryville. We never did find the top of the tank. Tanks like we had were welded in the middle. The bottom part of our tank was buried in the ground from the impact. The top of it, I guess, went straight to the moon!

The garage was set behind the house with a driveway leading down to it. All this happened during the time that we had the roofing business, so we kept a 500 gallon gas tank on each side of the driveway for fueling our trucks. It was so hot even 150 feet away from the burning garage building. Daddy made us get a water hose and walk from one tank to the other. I will never forget this. We actually had to bend down so the heat would not burn to our faces. It felt like our faces were frying. We watered those gas tanks down to keep them from blowing up. I was scared! I was terrified!

Here came the Law, the fire department and the neighbors! What a commotion!

When the police came, Daddy told them to leave. He shouted, "this is my fire and I'll fight it. The best thing for you to do is hit the road." That is what they did. The Law never messed with my Daddy. He used to call them, curse them out, and dare them to come get him. Occasionally, they would come and get him, bust his head, and throw him in the cruiser. They always brought him back home drunker than he was when they took him away.

Mama

Many times my daddy would beat my mama until they would have to rush her in an ambulance to the hospital to keep her alive. That is how badly he beat her over and over and over....

19

Once, daddy sent all of us down the mountain to pick poke salat. It was a trick to get rid of us. When we got to the bottom of the hill, we heard Mama screaming. We thought Daddy was killing her. By the time we got back to the house he had a knife and was trying to stab her. We all jumped on him but he would sling us under the table or knock us up against a wall. Finally, Daddy cooled down a little, and we all ran out of the house into the woods. I will never forget that day. Daddy had hit Mama between the eyes and a big knot had come up on her forehead. My heart went out to her because she was crying so pitifully. That day I found out what nerves could do...mine were tied in knots. I was jerking all over. There were neighbors within sight, but no one came to help. I guess they were just to scared to get involved with our problems.

Another time, we came in one evening after Mama had fixed us a beautiful meal. We all sat down. Then Daddy came in, grabbed Mama by the hair, and pulled her to the floor. Of course, our food went with her. On top of all this, Daddy yelled at Mama to clean up the mess. I cry as I recall this incident.

Daddy

Before we left Six-Mile, Daddy was having chest pains. They became worse until he had a heart attack that almost killed him. But Daddy was tougher than a coop rat. Although the doctors warned him to stop drinking and to slow down, he was in high gear all the time.

He woke up before daylight and began drinking whiskey. Daddy went to Knoxville to buy whiskey by the case. He carried it in his truck. Roy Hubbard (now deceased) had a store at the corner just below our house. Daddy stopped in one morning to see if Roy wanted anything (meaning whiskey) from Knoxville. Roy said that he did have a cold coming on and needed a bottle from Knoxville. Well, Daddy went to Knoxville, got a case, stopped at Roy's store and delivered the bottle.

"Daddy with his Moonshine Still"

"Mama" (front right)

The next morning Daddy was up bright and early. He returned to store and asked Roy for the bottle of whiskey back. Promising to bring Roy another one, Daddy turned up the fifth of whiskey and killed it straight. When it came to drinking whiskey, Daddy never needed a chaser of any kind. This fifth of whiskey taken back from Roy followed a whole case Daddy had gone through the night before.

It breaks my heart to talk about these things. But I believe with all my heart that God wants these remembrances recorded. I hope and pray that they will help somebody.

Street Lights

In one memory when I was about ten, I was in bed. My Daddy walked in and said, "wake up, boy." He handed me a pistol and a box of shells. He also had a pistol and I thought to my self, "what does this old drunk want now?"

He said, "let's go outside, boy. I can't sleep and that light is keeping me up."

We went outside and shot the pistols at the street light. We used more than a box of shells and never did hit the street light. I never did figure out why Daddy didn't just close his bedroom curtain to keep out the light.

With all of the shooting, the police showed up! They were always scared of my Daddy. When they saw that it was him, they kept right on going. They were not about to

25

pull into his driveway while he held a gun. When he saw them driving up the road, Daddy said, "go in there and get my shot gun, boy." I went in the house, got the pump shot gun, loaded it and brought it out. The law never did come back. It's a good thing, because Daddy would have shot them. That's the type of person my Daddy was.

Daddy's Death

After Mamaw died, Daddy always said he wanted to be buried "at the foot of Mamma." That is what he always said and that is exactly what happened. He is buried at the foot of his Mamma right here off Six-Mile at New Providence Church. Daddy died in 1975, five years later than Mamaw. Seemingly, he ran as hard and as fast as he could to get there. He never considered what he was leaving...his family and the opportunity to lead them in God's service. Dad died an alcoholic.

I praise God for the fact that Daddy did give his life to Jesus on his death bed. How much better his life would have been and how much better our life would have been if only he hadn't waited so long! What a difference Jesus' presence in our home would have made! Don't wait. Invite Jesus into your heart now!

Daddy's death bed experience was very unusual. Actually he died once and they revived him. Someone went for the preacher who led my Daddy to Jesus. Daddy told my uncle that he felt dirty all over. He actually stated, "I just feel nasty and dirty all over."

I believe he was talking about the inward spirit because after he had given his life to Jesus, he told my mama, "Joann I'm a changed person. When I go home, we are

27

going to hold a revival out at the house. I'm a different person! I feel good all over! I want to go home."

My mama told him, "Bud, you don't need to raise up out of bed. The doctor's told you to stay in bed."

Daddy said, "No, I'm going home!" When he raised up out of bed, his eyes sank back in his head, and he died. He went home, praise God, but he didn't go home with us. He went home with Jesus.

At that time, I hated my Daddy so much that I was actually thrilled because he had died. It just seemed like a burden lifted off me. He used to treat us so badly. We never got to watch TV. I do not ever recall doing any school work at home or getting any help or support of any kind. I made straight F's from the second to the ninth grade. They finally kicked me out of school. I think the reason they kept me as long as they did was that they were scared of me. I truly believed that all my troubles were Daddy's fault. So, when he died, I was glad.

At the same time, my brother, Donny, took daddy's death very hard. In my thirty-five years, I have never seen anyone take a death the way my brother, "Frog," took our daddy's death. When they told him that daddy had died, Frog just fell like a dish rag being slung to the floor. They revived him with smelling salt. As soon as he awoke and realized what had happened, he hit the floor again. He did that on and on and on…. He would vomit, cry, and moan. Daddy's death tore Donny's heart out while it made my heart glad. Even as I speak now, years later, I just can't believe how two brothers could react so differently to the same event.

I forgave my daddy for what he did to us. I really did. I love Daddy now. I believe he did the best he could with what he had. I just wish that he had found God earlier in his life. Without a doubt, Jesus could have gotten his life straightened out. But, Praise the Lord, Daddy is in heaven now. Someday, I'll see him again.

Six months after my daddy died, I began to miss him so badly it hurt. It just felt like something tore my heart out of my body. I can remember one time at Christmas. Mama walked in while I was sitting in a chair crying. Mama said, "what's wrong, son!"

I was on the phone trying to dial heaven. I was begging God to let me talk to my daddy. That's how much I missed him.

"Mama," I said, "I love Daddy, and I miss him." She talked to me and comforted me. That is about all she could do because she could not bring him back. Neither could I.

Escape

I had to leave Tennessee to get away from the needle, the bottle, and the old "friends." Things had become so bad that I would get into drugs belonging to my customers while I was out on a job. I would get into drugs at the homes of my friends. I would crush the drugs and run them up without knowing or caring if they killed me. I could not have cared less what happened to me. Before this time, I

31

never had the desire to live. I went to Atlanta, Georgia for five years. While in Atlanta, I did manage to get off the needle, but I was on booze even worse. Looking back, I can see that there was no escape and no refuge from the storm my life had become. Without Jesus, there can be no calm in any one's storm. Without him, there can be no peace that passes all understanding.

I had done every drug available. Drugs were my friend. When coming down from a high, I have clawed on the ground and foamed at the mouth like a mad dog for up to ten solid hours. With my so called "friend," this was all that life amounted to.

I now realize that Jesus is the way, the light, and the only true high people can have. Jesus can fill all voids with love, happiness, and peace. Praise God forever! Thank God for the blood of Jesus!

Dallas, Texas

I married and moved to Dallas, Texas when I was only 15 years old. We drove an old '57 Ford panel truck. This was just one leg of my journey down the road to ruin. We were going down there for work. I was just a young boy and had no business being married. The first thing I did in Texas was meet a murderer who lived next door to me. He and I smoked a joint together one day. That began a disastrous friendship. We went to town and began talking.

When we returned home, he got out of the car and said, "if you ever need anybody killed, just holler at me." I thought to my self, "what a joke!" He was a small boy who wore chrome shades and acted like he ruled the world. The next day he came over. As we talked, he showed me where he had been shot six times. I guess that toughened him up some despite his small size. The man who had shot him had freaked out on drugs so badly that he was just shooting at random. When my friend got out of the hospital he went to the gunman's house. He had his attacker down on the floor begging for his life. My friend loaded him in the vehicle and took him to a nearby park where he told him to get out of the vehicle. As the man got out begging for his life, my friend pumped the shotgun and shot him in the stomach over and over. The gun blast spun the man around and blew the whole back of his head off. This happened frighteningly close to our house.

After some time passed, this murderer and I started partying together. One night he came over and knocked on my door.

He said, "Flip, let's go bar hopping."

I said," let's go!" My wife had already left me and gone back to Tennessee.

My friend's brother-in-law walked up and said, "You can't go anywhere because if you go and get into trouble they'll come and get me because I'm your guardian."

My friend jerked a butcher knife out of his coat, jumped on his brother-in-law's back, and stabbed him down below his belt. It just ripped open.

As a kid growing up, I'd seen many a hog cut and killed, but I've never seen any cut like this before. The man lived, but it was only by the grace of God. Since I did not know God at that time, I just could not figure any way he could have survived that knifing. It was beyond my understanding. All of life was beyond my understanding at this point in my life. What was the use of going on if there was nothing different to look forward to?

Razor

I can remember another time when I was in my '57 Ford panel wagon. I had been drinking and doing drugs. I was around 17 years old when my first wife and I had a fight. I left and was going home. Well, that rage started up in side of me. The more I thought about it, the angrier I got. I was starting to go around a curve when I rammed the truck into second gear and held it to the floor. The truck spun all the way around in the road and slapped a light pole right behind my door. The impact slung the wagon about thirty feet in a ditch near a field. I tried to get out, but I was stuck. When it finally went forward, I went through six strings of barbed wire, five fence posts, a mail box and a corner post. There was so much wire that the wagon

36

stopped. I got my ball bat, got out and beat the wire off my vehicle. I got back, went back through the fence on my way out, drove home and got into bed.

The next morning the phone rang, and a man said, "Sparks, why didn't you wait on me to help you out last night?"

It looked like someone had taken a razor to me. I was cut all over. The hand of God had spared my life again. Praise His name.

REMEMBRANCES

Side one/Living life in the shadow of the cross

God's seed

The flip side of my story began when I first listened to God speak to me through a TV preacher whose name I do not even remember. It was one Sunday and I was alone in my apartment. I was on LSD acid when a preacher came on TV.

As I listened, I said to myself, "man, this dude makes a lot of since in a very messed up world."

God put his seed in me that day. Although there were still many rough times ahead of me (most of which were caused by my own back sliding and disobedience), I was very aware of God's presence with me. How I thank him for allowing me to know him. In case you wondered why side two precedes side one in my story, it is because I spent the first part of my life in the "unknown" area of life without Jesus. I was on my way to total destruction. How I wish I had known Jesus at a younger age. How I wish I had lived for him all my life.

A few more days went by after my first illumination. I was strung out on LSD acid again. Sitting in my apartment by myself a preacher came on TV again. The more I listened to him, the more I realized that he was the only person in the world who made any sense to me.

God began dealing with me that day in a very serious manner. God was tending the seed he had put in my heart.

I told him, "God, if you'll give me the strength just to make it back to Tennessee, I'll give you my life. Please let me get back home." Although I was on LSD acid and not in my right mind, that decision was the most soundest I have ever made. I thank the Lord that he came down in my apartment that day. Thank you Jesus! Praise his name for knowing in my heart that I meant my promise.

Coming Home

I went and got my brother, Frog, who lived nearby.

I said, "Frog, I'm going home."

He said, "well, let's go!"

As I started to pull out of Dallas, Texas in that old '57 Ford panel truck, it started missing, spitting, and sputtering. I only had enough gas money to get us home. I thought my world had come to an end, but we made it home. I was in the house of the Lord the next Sunday. I fell on the altar with brother, Ronny Regan. I genuinely gave my life to God.

My old rowdy biker friends hardly believed my new birth. They would tell people, "Old Flip has flipped out. He's done so many drugs that he's flipped plum out. He's lost his mind. He's talking about a man named Jesus now."

As time went on, I slid back. As the Bible says, I went seven times worse. Thank God, I returned home to him! I thank Jesus for sparing my life. I hope that some how He will help me to help others. Time goes by fast. We have not got a lot of time in life. There are a lot of people out there that we need to reach with the good news of Jesus Christ and his love. My goal in life is to help people. I just hope and pray that some how God will let me have a enough strength and enough wisdom to be able to do that. With out Him, I was/am nothing. With Him I can do anything!

Randy and Roger

My good friends Randy Peaks, Roger Riddle, a few others, and myself were getting drunk one night. Randy had gone to town that day and bought himself some new clothes. I will never forget the shirt he had on that night. It had a devil holding a pitch fork. The shirt said, "Going Down!"

Randy and I were taking and getting pretty loose.

He said to me, "Flip, this will be the last cigarette I smoke."

I thought that it was time for me to go because I was not in any mood to hear a lot of pity that night. You know how a bunch of drunks can be. I left the party early.

You know, I wonder if Randy somehow knew that he was going to die.

As they drove home, they went around a curve and hit a tree. The wreck killed two of the four boys in the car, including Randy. God spared two of their lives. I am glad to say that they are both Christians now. Do we ever wonder what our last words will be? God help us!

Cold

It got rough during the recession of the '70's. There was no work to be found. I can remember lying in bed.

43

There was no hot water because the water heater had blown up. We did not have any heat. I had to lay in that little bed with all the socks and clothes I could pile on to keep from freezing to death. Back then, winter was winter. When there is no heat in the house, winter hurts!

Beans

All we had to eat was beans. An older cousin and I were eating beans and something popped. It was my cousin's tooth breaking.

He said, "Flip, did you not wash the beans?"

"Why no," I said, "They came in a pack. You don't have to wash those things when they come in a pack like that."

He said, "Dadgumit, you do, too! Let Onion make the beans from now on."

"All right," I said, "That'll be alright with me."

My cousin said, "that Onion makes a good pack of beans."

So I said, "I'll let Onion cook all the time."

Then Onion said, "well, I never wash the beans either."

Bad to Worse

Since Daddy's death, everything had changed. Mama went to work to support the family. When she was gone, we attempted to raise ourselves, and we did a mighty poor job of it. We had some rough times during which my brothers and I did little to make things easier for Mama.

Finally, she could not take it anymore. Mama moved out, married Don Taylor and let us have the old house.

It wasn't that Mama didn't care for us. She was a beautiful person, and she had proven her love for us many times. Enduring the abuse she suffered in order to stay home with us was more than anyone should have borne. Unfortunately, after Daddy died, it just seemed like the devil came into our lives with all the force he had. We were completely out of control.

I stayed at Chilhowee Lake in the '70's. That's when the police had the paddy wagon. I remember that they used to come and get us in that paddy wagon time after time. With gangs like Smoke Riders, Mountain Rebels, Hell's Angels, Outlaws, etc. we all just stayed so stoned out of our brains we did not know the ground we walked on. I can remember times when I was doped up for days and days. I would beg and steal...whatever I had to do to get high.

Brother

By this time I was looking to my older brother for help...but no help came. Ronny would take us to concerts and parties. One weekend, he took us to a ZZ Top concert and gave us drugs. Those drugs almost killed me. I got down on my hands and knees and crawled out of that place. At that time, Ronny was into women and not younger brothers. Although I idolized him, he never knew it. Ronny would stay gone for days or even weeks on bike runs. I was a very confused thirteen-year-old and more alone than ever.

Soon after Daddy's death, Ronny went to prison for 10 years. So, there went my brother.

In my quest for drugs, my first cousin, Moody, and I would break in and steal drugs from houses we knew to have them. Once we heard of a place with five hundred horse tranquilizers. We took them and stayed high for a long time. My cousin took five of the pills one morning while sitting out back of the house rolling a joint. Well, when he finally came to himself, he was still sitting on that stump behind the house. All day long he sat there staring somewhere into space. We all thought that was really cool, although Moody never did get his joint rolled. He just sat there.

Bikers

Most of the guys I started hanging out with were bikers. I could ride away from home on a cycle and stay gone for days. All I wanted was to stay wherever there were drugs and parties.

I partied with the Smoke Riders up in Tallahassee, Tennessee, which is in Happy Valley. We often went to the Valley and partied for days with the Outlaws and Hell's Angels. Life was one big party and then, things got worse.

School

Since the age of thirteen I had owned a vehicle. My first one, a '56 Ford Royal Crown, was one in which I have pulled and fixed the transmission and the motor.. It seemed only natural to drive to school. After all, I was drinking by the age of thirteen, why not drive?

I can remember going to school with a pint of whiskey in each boot. Because I stayed drunk at school, no one would mess with me. I went to school only to pass out on my desk and stay passed out class after class. When I did wake up, I would realize that everyone had gone and left me behind. Somehow, I would struggle from class to class and collapse in every one of them. Unconsciousness was such a welcome relief from reality.]

Close Call

Back then, I never knew anything about God. Nobody ever told me about Jesus and how Jesus loved me. I thank God for not letting me die in my sins. The boy who overdosed me when I was 12 is now dead. He took the same amount of drugs I took and was a lot older than I was. He was the one who gave drugs to me. They took him to the hospital and pumped his stomach. He survived that ordeal, but later he and his sister burned in a car wreck together. The high I shared with him left me laid out in a field under an old-40-something model car for two days. I was so doped up I should have died, but it was God's will that I didn't.

About everything that could be imagined has happened to me in my life. I wanted to be like my daddy. After he died, I missed him so much it hurt me. I just wanted to stay drunk and beat up just as many people as I could. That is exactly what I did.

Following Daddy

I can remember times I went around for hours and days without knowing the world around me. I would actually foam at the mouth like a mad dog. I would lie around on the ground kicking and crying like a baby. I fell into the same steps my daddy walked in and I did not even realize that it was happening.

Time went on. I got in the roofing business just like my Daddy did. Worked from daylight until dark. I worked like I was fighting fire. I worked like there wasn't going to be a tomorrow. Somehow, I wanted my daddy to be proud of me and he wasn't even around. I wanted people that knew me to know that my daddy was Bud Sparks. Daddy was my hero when I was growing up although I was terrified of him. After he was dead, Daddy turned out to be my best friend. I worshipped the ground he had walked on. I had never taken flowers to Daddy's grave. Instead, I busted many a whiskey bottle on his grave while I was drunk. Many times I wrecked my vehicle before I could drive to his grave. I almost died in car wrecks. I have wrecked every vehicle I ever owned.

Jeff Sparks

Cheating Death

There were hundreds of times that by all human calculations I should have died. The first was early in life when I first began learning to what extent abuse was prominent in my family. After Donny was born, Mama told me how she would often have Ronny take us kids to Mamaw's for safety. She told him that she would follow later. It was then that Mama suffered terribly from Daddy's cruelty. After one of these times, Mama took a gun into the bedroom intending to kill herself. As she recounted the incident to us…suddenly the room lit up like a bright star, and someone said, "there will be better days. Don't do it!"

As I look back now (from my better days), I realize that Mama had to go to heaven to see her better days. On Earth, she was treated like dirt and beaten to the very death's door many times.

Remember how young I was at this time, and yet death, fear, and pain were already trailing me. Often, I had to run from trouble at school. In those days (1960's) racial troubles were bad. I was the only white boy in my kindergarten class. Talk about fear... I had it!

While I was still a bow legged boy, eating dirt from the flowerbeds, I knew when my daddy came home drunk and beat my Mama. At this young age, he also took me to bars. I was terrified, because there was a sense of fear and hate in those places.

In Midway, Ohio there was a lake called Crystal Lake. In the winter it was so cold that the lake froze. While we waited for the school bus, the older kids skated on the lake. I decided I would skate, too. However, I fell through a hole in the ice and could have died.

I believe God has a mission for each person even while he/she is in the mother's womb. It was not my time to leave Earth although I found myself below the surface of an icy lake. God wanted me to live.

One time I wrecked a vehicle in the dead, cold heart of winter, twenty-six degrees below zero. I was so drunk I could not walk. I went over an embankment and landed next to a creek. The car was on its side. The boys were with me. We smelled gasoline and got out of the vehicle. As I was standing by the door of the car I slipped off in a ditch and fell into the creek. Remember that it was twenty-six degrees below zero. I was so drunk that I actually lost my companions. I was wondering around in a daze, lost for over an hour.

I finally did make it back out of the woods, but it was surely by the grace of God. When I made it to the road, my clothes were frozen to my body. Feeling like I was already frozen, I was getting ready to lay down on the side of the road and give it up...just go to sleep. Then I saw some headlights. A friend stopped and took me home. That is just one time out of hundreds that God graciously saved my life. He had already spared my life many times in vehicles with Daddy while he was still alive. Now, He continued saving me.

My Bridge

Another time at Chilhowee View School, there was a narrow one-lane bridge. They should have dedicated that bridge to me. I went through it in a blackout running over eighty miles an hour. This happened after driving over 100 miles an hour through back streets on Battle Branches curvy roads. I was so drunk that I thought I was racing another man I hated. As it turned out, this racer was not the man I was out to get. The man I was racing stopped at a store. He came up to me as I was coming out of the blackout. Then I realized that he was not the person I thought he was. People said I had been chasing him backward around the gas pumps, smoking the tires and trying to run over him.

As I left the store, I headed down the road. I went through the little bridge, bouncing off the walls. It was just as if Jesus grabbed me and shook me to wake me up.

Jesus said to me, "son, you're a wreck." I laid down in the seat and hit first a cedar tree and then a rock wall. It demolished the vehicle. Actually, the crash did enough damage to total four vehicles.

When I woke up, the door was jammed. I realized I had to get out of there, because the Law was coming. After several trys, I did make it out of the vehicle. When I hit the ground, it knocked me out again. For several minutes, I kept losing and regaining consciousness. Once I passed out in the middle of the road as I was trying to run. The next thing I knew, a man was shaking me to wake me. I can remember chasing him away. I intended to whip him if he did not leave me alone.

He finally said, "son, you've got to go to the hospital. You're in bad shape."

I ran him off, got up and ran back down the road.

Because I had lost a lot of blood, I was weak. I dragged myself over an embankment. Here came the law and ambulances! People were everywhere!

I thought out loud, "boy, I've tripped them up good again. I'm going to the house and lie down and go to sleep."

Something or someone said to me," Flip, you're in bad shape, Son. You've got to get to a hospital." I wiped my hand across my face. There were just streams and clots of blood coming from my mouth and nose.

The Struggle

I thought, "oh, my goodness!"

Slowly, I crawled back up the bank into the road. Someone threw me on a stretcher, rushed me into an ambulance and buckled me down. As I woke, I was demanding to be let out and allowed to go home. The lady who was attending me gave me a strong, "No!"

In all God's honesty, that made me so mad that I broke the straps on the stretcher. Those straps are made of the same stuff as vehicle seat belts. I still have an indention on my leg where the strap was. At this point the police jumped in to restrain me.

I will never forget the look on the ambulance attendant's face. She said, "son, do you want to die?"

I said, "no, I don't want to die."

Then she answered, "if you don't lay here and let me suction the blood out of your nose, you're a dead man because you're hemorrhaging."

I woke up under an operating light. They were using a scalpel to dig glass and torn flesh out of my mouth. Since I was so drunk they did not give me anything for the pain. You can imagine how I wanted to whip the doctor and kick his head off because I was hurting badly. I was still drunk but not drunk enough to stop the pain.

In the background I could hear someone calling my name. "Sparks… Sparks… Sparks." I looked around, and there were two officers waiting for me.

"Are you ready to go?" They asked.

"Go where?" Was my question.

They replied, "you're going to jail."

My answer was, "no, sir, you're wrong. I'm staying right here in the hospital. I'm hurt. You're not taking me nowhere."

The officer said, "no, you've got to go to jail."

I challenged, "come on over here and get me."

The officer then said, "Sparks, now let's talk this over."

I repeated, "no, come on over here and get me."

Then all my bravo left me. I broke down and cried like a little kid. I could not believe I had wrecked my truck, gone out and gotten drunk, then wrecked my vehicle again. Unfortunately, that never broke me from the drug habit. This drug abuse went on and on and on like a broken record…. Never ending. All I wanted was more whiskey and more drugs. Things got worse and worse. I could never get enough. I began to get strung out on a needle. I have done every drug there is to do. I have eaten bottles full of Valium. I have wrecked every vehicle. Why did it take me so long to learn?

Mama's Death

I just thought that I had my rough times after my Daddy died. I thought things were going to get calmed down. I thought things were really going to look up. Then, my Mama was murdered. You know, a couple of days before

Mama's death I told her, "Mama, I'll give you some money. You can put it in the bank if it'll make you feel better. If you'll quit your job and answer the phone for my business, Mama, I'll pay you."

I would have paid her well, too. God knows that I loved her more than anything in this world. I loved my Mama. She agreed to come and work with me. Mama turned in her notice on a Monday, and she was going to quit on the following Friday.

I agreed to give her one thousand dollars that would have been paid on the Friday after she had quit her job. She agreed to do that. I was just tickled to death, because I wanted to take care of my Mama. On Tuesday of that week, Mama was working out her one week notice, when my brother, Donny, killed her. You know, I would not kill a dog the way that my brother killed my Mama. It tore the

65

heart out of my body. This was the hardest thing I have ever gone through. Donny shot my Mama. He shot her six times. I had called Mama to warn her that I felt something was wrong. I told her to lock her doors and not let anybody in the house. I told her not to let Frog in, because he had gone crazy.

People at the store told me Frog had come in asking for shells. They would not sell him any at the Foothills store. They said he was the devil with a cold look in his eyes. I had a job to estimate in Maryville, so I called Mama from a phone booth.

I said, "Mama, don't let Donny in the house. Mama, I'll get there as quickly as I can."

I had to go meet the man at Child Kingdom in Maryville about a roofing job. I went up there as fast as I could. I went back home and started to go to Mama's when the phone rang.

This man told me, "Son your daddy needs you over here. Don't bring nobody with you. Hurry over here."

I got mad and said, "Buddy, I don't know who you are, and I hope I don't find out who you are. Don't you ever call my house again." I continued, "My daddy's dead. Don't ever call here again."

The man came back on the phone and said, "Your step-daddy needs you, now!" I thought to myself, "My God! What went wrong? He's killed Don." I really thought my brother had killed my step-daddy. I knew something bad was wrong, but I had no idea just how bad it was.

My brother, Donny, had walked up to Mama. She asked him, "Son, what have you got!"

He pulled a gun out of his back pocket and shot my Mama in the arm. Then he walked closer to her. Mama put her hands up over her face. Donny took the gun, put it up to her hands, and blew her brains out. My God! He crucified her. He didn't stop even then. Donny shot four more times into Mama's head. My life was over! My life was over!

After Mama had gone through that living hell and now she was dead. My own flesh and blood brother killed my Mama after all the hell she went through to raise both of us. After all the beatings that she got in her life for us…. This was her reward!?

My mama could have left us earlier, but she didn't. She stayed with us, because she loved us. Now she was dead. I could not stand to look at the way she died. It was more than I could take. I did not want to be around anybody. I hated everybody.

They took me to the hospital and the old faithful drugs were there. They shot me up with a full syringe of Phenergan and Morphine and /or Phenergan and Demerol to get me out of my misery. Escape was all I could think of. I felt as if my life was over. After they doped me up, my oldest brother, Ronny, helped them carry me out of that place. They gave me a prescription for Phenergan and Morphine. We went to the drug store and got the prescriptions filled. Before I walked out of the door of that place, I had taken the lid off the bottles and swallowed thirty of the pills. I did not tell Ronny what I had just done.

I went to my house and killed a fifth of whiskey. I did every kind of drug I could get my hands on. The next day, I called the hospital and told them I had lost my prescriptions. I took over thirty more Phenergan and Morphine tablets. At that time my brother was giving me other drugs right and left. All I had to do was hold out my hand. By the next day I had eaten over eighty pills. Then the hospital found out what I was doing. They called to advise me that if I went to sleep, I would never wake up. For days I was in a doped up blackout.

Funeral

You know, at my mama's funeral, God knows I'll never forget this, I came to myself. I looked and saw my brothers and sister all up front crying. The family was at the front of

70

the church and I was back with the rest of the people. I didn't know the world I walked in. I came to myself and made my way to my Mama's casket. I was rubbing her head when a man who did not know who I was came up to me.

He said, "Son, don't be rubbing her head. Her heads liable to cave in."

Oh man! Lord Jesus! I could've killed him. I could've killed him deader than four o'clock for saying that. My God! That tore my heart out.

"Frog"

Time went on. I would have killed Donny if I could have gotten a hold of him. I intended to take dynamite, wire

71

it to the bumper of my truck and go down off Court Street in Maryville with the accelerator wide open and hit the court house with the ten-ton load of rock that was on my truck. I meant to kill them all. I fully intended to kill anybody and everybody who got in my path that day.

But, there was a little something in my heart saying, "Don't do that, Flip. Don't kill all those innocent people."

So I thought about strapping dynamite to myself and walking in there to tell everybody else to leave. Then, I would kill my self, and I would kill Donny, too. Some how, I just never found it in my heart to carry out this plan.

My brother had lived with me in Atlanta for five years. All that time I knew Donny was sick. I had even had him committed to mental institutions. I was always scared of

Donny. He had light blue eyes with a look in them that was of the devil. Some times you could look into those eyes and know that nobody was really at home inside him. This made him a spooky person. Weighing about two hundred fifty pounds made him a big boy and gave him the advantage when he and I fought. In fact, he broke every rib in my body one time just by falling on me.

Yes, I knew Donny was seriously troubled but I never dreamed he would kill my Mama. I always thought if he ever killed anybody-that anybody would be me. I had asked his doctor one time if she thought that I would be the one killed if Donny ever reached that point.

She had told me, "he'll kill the one he loves the most."

My God! That is what he did! He had killed Mama. You can never imagine the agony I suffered unless it has

73

Jeff Sparks

happened to you. I pray to God that it will not happen to anyone. Through all the abuse (sexual, drug, physical, mental, etc.) and after all those years Donny, snapped and killed his own Mama. Jesus help him!

Trashing My Home

There are a lot more incidents that have happened to me...too many to mention. There were times when I got drunk and actually broke every thing in my house. I would go into a violent rage and just kick, stomp, rant and rave. I have kicked chairs and tables completely through walls and did not even know it until the next day. Later, my foot would hurt me so bad that it would wake me up at night. I had broken every bone in my right foot by kicking stuff and busting it. When I open the doors of my trailer, I saw things

74

ripped out. I would try to figure out what happen, because every thing I owned was out side in a pile. I could not understand what had happened. I just could not gain a hold of myself. It was hard to realize what I had done.

Hope in Jesus

I pray that the telling of these remembrances will somehow make sense to any and all who read this book. I want to help young people. I laid my life down. The times when I lived without Jesus was useless. Most of my people are dead and gone. The only good that can ever come from theses written memories is that readers will realize there own need for God. I do not want anyone to suffer a life like mine.

75

Jeff Sparks

Now, I have Jesus in my life, and he will be with me forever. I would not trade anything for Jesus. His presence has made all the difference in the world to me. I backslid on the Lord a couple of times, but He has *never* left me. With God's grace and mercy I pray that this remembrance book will somehow help others and keep them from taken the dead-end road on which I traveled for to long. "Living Life in a Living Hell" would have to be the title to the collection of remembrances covering my life before Jesus. Once He came to live in my heart, everything changed.

Life before the Lord was filled with nothing but trouble. I have had all the hepatitis diseases you can have-A, B, C... all of it. I could have been dead long ago. Almost every bone in my body has been broken from fighting and kicking. I have been shot, cut, spit on, and otherwise mistreated more than once. I just thank God that he spared my life until I realized who He was.

Invitation

If you do not know Jesus personally, He stands at your heart's door waiting to be invited inside. Only you can invite Him inside. Once Jesus enters your life, things will be better for you. God has good things planned for his children.

Jeff Sparks

Epilogue

After I gave my life to Jesus for the first time, I was cutting paper wood near where I now live off Six-Mile. I will never forget this. I was by myself when I walked up to a creek. I was married at the time and cutting wood for a living. I was just a young man, but I thought how peaceful and quiet it was while I was standing by that creek. I looked up at Chilhowee Mountain and said, "God, it's so beautiful here. I'd give anything if I had a home here with some land that had a creek like this flowing across it." I wanted my home dead in the middle of my land. To me that was an unattainable dream at the time. But, you know, that same creek where I was standing turned out to be the creek that runs through property I bought just over the fence. God allowed me to buy five acres of land twenty years after I talked to Him about it. It still amazes me that the same creek (where I described my dream place to God) runs through the property He allowed me to own. God is so wonderful! Why do we forget that He already owns *all* property, *all* creeks, and *all* mountains?

God brought this dream back to my remembrance recently. With the dream now realized, I thought, "Precious Jesus! How Beautiful" How much more of a God could a person want? What other God could/would give the desires of our hearts that way? Although it took twenty years because of my own detours through backsliding and drugs, Jesus answered my prayers. How I thank Him for it.

I now have a wife, Leann, and two beautiful little girls, Vanessa Hope and Kristen Lace. We have sold that place by the creek, but still live on the same mountain just up the street from my dream place. God is allowing us to prosper. We have built a new home and are getting ready to sell it. I just pray that the money I make building and selling homes can be used to help people.

Indeed, if the first part of my remembrance book were titled, "Living Life in a Living Hell" (without Jesus), the later part of the same book would bare the title, "Living Life in the Shadow of the Cross" (with Jesus). My story is like the hit songs recorded on vinyl discs of years past. On the main side (side one) one could purchase the desired hit song of the day. However, on the flip side (side two) recording companies put unknown songs. The main side of anyone's life is when he/she loves and walks with God. The flip side of any person's life is that he/she spends trying to live without Him. Worse than any "unknown" song, this time spent living in sin leads only to destruction.

It is my sincere hope that the Lord will allow me to serve Him for many years. As I walk with Him gathering remembrances, perhaps someday I will be able to add many more to this account. Hopefully the second side-side one of my life's story-the main part (time spent with Jesus) will be much longer than side two-the first part of my life (time spent hopelessly trying to survive without Him). How I wish I had known Jesus all of my life. As Dallas Holm said in one of his wonderful song, "If I had it to do all over again, I'd serve Jesus everyday of my life."

What a difference Jesus made in my life! What a difference he longs to make in yours!

"THANKS BE TO GOD FOR HIS UNSPEAKABLE

GIFT!"

(2 Corinthians 9:15)

Jeff "Flip" Sparks and his wife, Leann

References

Cross, Phil. "Jesus built a Bridge," Phil Cross/Cameron Hill Music/ Chris White Music, sunlight Records, BMI< Nashville, Tennessee, 1993. (Citation on p.4

Daniel, W.H. and Bernice M. Bostrom. "In the Shadow of the Cross." Favorite Songs and Hymns. Stamps Baxter Music Co. Chattanooga, Tennessee, 1938. (Citation on p.38)

Holm, Dallas. "If I Had It To Do All Over Again." Dallas Holm & Praise Live-Rise Again. Dimension Music/SESAC, R3723, Greentree Records a division of

Jeff Sparks

Benson Company, Inc., Nashville, Tennessee, 1978. (Citation on p.36)

Landon, Michael. Little House on the Prairie. Film series base on Books by Laura Ingalls Wilder. National Broadcasting Co., Inc. 1974. (Citation on p.1)

Old song cited on page 9-Composer unknown Scripture reference taken from the Authorized (King James) Version of the Holy Bible

About the Author

The author is presently residing outside Maryville, Tennessee with his wife, Leanna, and their daughters, Kristen and Vanessa. The Lord has greatly blessed him. Mr. Sparks operates his own successful excavating business and builds houses to sell. In the near future, Mr. Sparks plans to complete toward full contractor's license.

Jeff and his family attend the Mountain View Church of God in Maryville, Tennessee where he is greatly inspired by his pastor's leadership, especially through a food bank Pastor Shubert has established. This sharing ministry blesses many people in the church and the community. Mr. Sparks is currently seeking God's will regarding a mountain retreat location to include cottages (which he will build) and a food bank. Mr. Sparks plans to utilize competent staff personnel to help rehabilitate and disciple people in need. With God's help, the staff can help solve spiritual, physical, emotional, and mental problems, and needs will be met according to God's riches in glory by Christ Jesus.

Jeff describes his present life situation in the following words: "I am alive, well, enjoying the blessings of God, and living in beautiful East Tennessee. I don't reckon a man can do any better."